Gray Foxes

by Jane P. Gardner

Consultant:
Blaire Van Valkenburgh
Professor
UCLA Department of Ecology and Evolutionary Biology

BEARPORT
PUBLISHING

New York, New York

Credits

Cover and Title Page, © Ken Canning/iStockphoto; 4–5, © Scenic Shutterbug/Shutterstock; 6–7, © Pete Oxford/DanitaDelimont.com/Danita Delimont Photography/Newscom; 8–9, © Jupiterimages/Getty Images/Photos.com/Thinkstock; 10, © lightpoet/Shutterstock; 10–11, © NHPA/SuperStock; 12–13, © Ron Sanford/Photo Researchers/Getty Images; 14–15, © imagebroker.net/SuperStock; 16–17, © Stone Nature Photography/Alamy; 18–19, © Scenic Shutterbug/Shutterstock; 20–21, 22T, © iStockphoto/Thinkstock; 22C, © Scenic Shutterbug/Shutterstock; 22B, © Jupiterimages/Getty Images/Photos.com/Thinkstock; 23T, © Scenic Shutterbug/Shutterstock; 23C, © Ron Sanford/Photo Researchers/Getty Images; 23B, © lightpoet/Shutterstock.

Publisher: Kenn Goin
Senior Editor: Joyce Tavolacci
Creative Director: Spencer Brinker
Design: Emily Love
Photo Researcher: Arnold Ringstad

Library of Congress Cataloging-in-Publication Data

Gardner, Jane P.
 Gray foxes / by Jane P. Gardner.
    p. cm. — (Wild canine pups)
 Audience: 6–9.
 Includes bibliographical references and index.
 ISBN 978-1-61772-931-7 (library binding) — ISBN 1-61772-931-0 (library binding)
 1. Gray fox—Infancy—Juvenile literature. 2. Foxes—Infancy—Juvenile literature. I. Title.
 QL737.C22G3734 2014
 599.775—dc23
                                    2013008958

For more information, write to Bearport Publishing Company, Inc., 45 West 21st Street, Suite 3B, New York, New York 10010. Printed in the United States of America.

10 9 8 7 6 5 4 3 2 1

❧ Contents ❧

Meet a gray fox kit

A baby gray fox darts in and out of a hollow log.

She uses sharp **claws** on her back feet to climb on top of it.

She is learning how to climb trees.

Nearby, the **kit**'s mother watches her closely.

What is a gray fox?

Gray foxes are part of the **canine** family.

They are about the size of a medium pet dog.

Gray foxes have thick fur and bushy tails.

Even though they are called gray foxes, their fur can be white, red, or black.

The foxes' fur keeps them warm when it is cold outside.

bushy tail

Adult gray fox size

Where do gray foxes live?

Gray foxes live in forests in North America and South America.

They make their homes, called **dens**, inside hollow logs or in the ground.

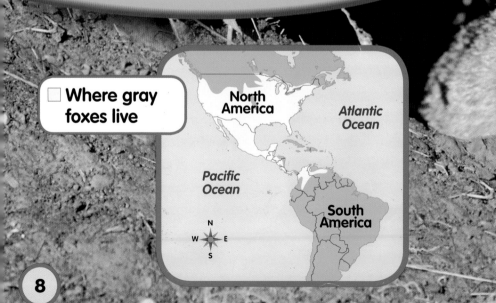

☐ Where gray foxes live

North America

Atlantic Ocean

Pacific Ocean

South America

N
W · E
S

When it is cold or rainy, foxes stay inside their dens.

Mother foxes also raise their babies inside dens.

kits at opening
to den

Tree homes

Sometimes, gray foxes make their dens high up in hollow trees.

Their tree dens can be 30 feet (9 m) off the ground!

There, foxes are safe from **predators**, such as wolves.

wolf

gray fox
in tree

Fox families

Gray foxes usually live alone.

In the fall, however, male foxes find females to **mate** with.

After mating, the two foxes live together in the forest.

In the spring, the mother fox gives birth to her babies in the den.

gray fox looking for mate

Newborn kits

Gray fox mothers usually have about four tiny kits.

At first, the newborns cannot even see their mother.

They are born with their eyes tightly closed.

When they are ten days old, their eyes open.

young kits
in den

15

Time to eat

At first, kits drink milk from their mother's body.

After three weeks, they eat food that their father brings.

The father finds fruit and catches mice, birds, and other small animals.

Then he carries the food back to the den to feed his babies.

kit drinking milk

Finding food

When they are four months old, gray fox kits learn to hunt.

Their father shows them how to leap on animals to catch them.

After a few lessons, the kits are ready to hunt on their own.

kit leaping

Growing up

Gray fox families stay together until the kits are ten months old.

Then the grown-up foxes leave their family.

Some choose to live far away.

However, most will stay close to where they were raised.

Some will find a treetop den in which to raise a new fox family!

grown-up
gray fox

21

Glossary

canine (KAY-nyen) related to the dog family, which includes pet dogs, wolves, and gray foxes

claws (KLAWZ) hard, sharp nails on the fingers or toes of an animal

dens (DENZ) homes where wild animals can rest, hide from enemies, and have babies

kit (KIT)
a baby fox

mate (MAYT)
to come
together to
have young

predators (PRED-uh-turz)
animals that hunt and
eat other animals

Index

Read more

Owen, Ruth. *Arctic Fox Pups (Wild Baby Animals)*. New York: Bearport (2011).

Swanson, Diane. *Foxes (Welcome to the World Series)*. Vancouver, BC: Whitecap Books (2010).

Learn more online

To learn more about gray foxes, visit
www.bearportpublishing.com/WildCaninePups

About the author

Jane P. Gardner is a freelance science writer with a master's degree in geology. She worked as a science teacher for several years before becoming a writer. She has written books about science, geography, history, and math.